BATTLE'S BLUEPRINT

5 Self Battles to Defeat for Success

BATTLE'S BLUEPRINT

5 Self Battles to Defeat for Success

NICHOLAS BATTLE

Foreword by: Charlynda Scales

2020

Battle's Blueprint: 5 Self Battles to Defeat for Success

NinosCorner Productions LLC

First Printing: 2020

Publishing Editor: Anne Steinbock of Cambridge Proofreading & Editing LLC

Cover Design: Shane Rounce

Instagram: @NinosCorner
Twitter: @NinosCorner
Facebook: @TheNinosCorner

Website: www.NinosCorner.com
Email: TheNinosCorner@gmail.com

ISBN 978-1-7333570-3-6 (Hardcover)
ISBN 978-1-7333570-4-3 (Paperback)
ISBN 978-1-7333570-5-0 (Ebook)

Dedication

To my grandfather, Edward Earl Brown…

I would not be the man I am today without your guidance.

Although I know you are looking at me from Heaven as I type

this, I wish you were still alive today to see how your

influences and teachings have made me the successful man I

am today.

Thank you for everything PawPaw. I would have never

accomplished any of this without you.

Contents

Foreword

At the beginning of 2015, I found myself staring at yet another piece of paper that would completely change my life. I made the decision to separate from active duty after serving proudly in the United States Air Force for over a decade. The next chapter of my life was calling—entrepreneurship.

It took me a few years of painstakingly living a double life to get brave enough to make the leap.

I was torn between comfort and my *calling*. This became a cyclical theme on my path to success with owning Mutt's Sauce, LLC.

My grandfather, a Korean and Vietnam War Air Force veteran, left in his will a piece of paper for a sauce recipe that he made in 1956. The value I placed on this gesture, this piece of paper, was the catalyst to everything that happened thereafter.

In the six years of running the company, I found myself reflecting on all of the divergent moments. The highs and the "rock bottom" moments were all necessary parts of the journey. While most will learn this with no "reg" or regulation, as we are used to having in the military, Nick Battle has masterfully summed up how to prepare for these moments in *Battle's Blueprint.*

Nick Battle is the one man I know who's lived up to his name. I met him over a decade ago. We were both newly commissioned Air Force officers at Warner Robins Air Force Base, Georgia.

We were not only friends, but *Battle Buddies.* I admired his integrity, relentless work ethic and intellect, which was consistent in his life, on and off duty.

I watched with pride as he rose through the ranks, served with grace and set the bar high everywhere he was stationed. As his friend, I also saw him defeat multiple personal battles, which earned my highest respect.

Through it all, he remained selfless, as evidence by this book. This is the guidebook I wish I had when I transitioned out of the military into entrepreneurship, and throughout my life.

May *Battle's Blueprint* be a positive catalyst in your life, as Nick Battle's presence has been in mine.

Charlynda Scales
Servant Leader & CEO
Mutt's Sauce LLC

x

Introduction

What is success and how do you accomplish it? Growing up, I was taught five principles that are the cornerstone to my personal and entrepreneurial successes. These ideologies are the basis and foundation of a successful life as represented by most successful people that surround me.

As a military officer, these blueprints to success have guided me in accomplishing many milestones, at home and while deployed to Afghanistan and Iraq. As a small business owner, these philosophies have launched me to success in establishing a "self-made" brand across three different industry platforms. As a hardworking individual, these models have led me to become the best father, son, and husband possible.

Battle's Blueprint is essential to becoming a winner in life, whether by achieving on-the-job success, garnering entrepreneurial accomplishments, or attaining many triumphs throughout the challenges life can hand you.

WIN THE BATTLE...WIN THE WAR...ACHIEVE SUCCESS

BLUEPRINT #1: Do Not Be Afraid to Fail

Dream it, prepare for it, and "do" it. Do not be afraid to fail. You can never expect greatness from yourself if you are afraid of disappointment.

HAVE YOU EVER WANTED TO CHASE your dreams and try to turn your vision into a reality, but never pursued your passion because of fear? As the days, months and years passed by, did you regret not attempting this action?

Well, I have some good and bad news for you. The good news is that you are not alone. We have all succumbed to the pressure of fear and allowed it to deter us from accomplishing a milestone. The bad news is, once you postpone your initial attempt to accomplish your task, you will more than likely never revisit any future attempts to pursue your vision.

Everyone dreams of being successful. But far too many people do not put in the necessary work to accomplish their vision and the goals they have set forth for themselves.

Once you "Dream" your goal, it is now time to begin preparation to achieve it. In order to prepare for your dream, you must learn as much about your goal as possible. Review similar success patterns accomplished in the fields you are interested in. Construct an outline or plan to chart your timeline to completion. Set milestones to give yourself a sense of achievement and accomplishment throughout the process. And, as stated earlier, continue to learn your craft. Knowledge is key.

Throughout this process, you will have failures along the way; expect it, because no plan is devoid of flaws. Do not be disappointed if things do not progress as you think they should. Plan for the worse, but work towards achieving the best. Moreover, never allow the fear of failure to drive you into paralysis. These key tenets will assure that your plan is as fail-proof as possible.

Adjust to the surprises life throws at you. What you currently deem as a failure may ultimately become one of your greatest successes.

Surprises happen in life, and the way you handle them is key to the measure of success and effectiveness you will obtain. To be successful, you need to navigate a positive path through the challenges a surprise may hand you. Adapting to the changes these surprises will deliver is a trait necessary to adhere to a high-quality and successful life.

Adjusting to surprises is not just accepting the change and moving on. Instead, if you know that this "surprise" will last for an extended period of time, you must embrace it to fully succeed. When I say embrace, I'm not telling you to accept the surprise with no reservations. I'm merely suggesting that you accept the challenges that come with it and focus on the positive aspects the surprise will give you. There's no need to reflect on the negative aspects, especially if the surprise is permanent and here to stay.

Concentrating on the positive factors will allow you to build a level of confidence within yourself concerning the way you handle the surprise; whether it is an unplanned event within your life or a failed attempt at accomplishing a task.

BATTLE'S BLUEPRINT

Knowing how to truly accept this surprise and work to foster an environment necessary to be successful in spite of the surprise will cultivate a level of confidence within yourself. Knowing that your deemed "failure" is something that you can overcome will lead you to accomplishments and greatness.

You have to learn to become *comfortable* being *uncomfortable*. When life throws you a challenge, you must strive to overcome the obstacles presented to you.

To become successful, you must step out of your comfort zone and apply pressure to yourself to succeed. Nothing in life is easy. As the old saying goes, "Pressure busts pipes"…but it also produces diamonds. How would you withstand the pressures of life? What category do you fall in?

If you want to become a medical doctor, there are many levels of uncomfortable pressure to the process that will test your comfortability. First off, you must earn a bachelor's degree, followed by receiving a competitive score on the Medical College Admissions Test. Next, you must be accepted to medical school and earn a medical degree. Once you have completed all this, you must then complete a residency program. You more than likely will not become a doctor until your early to mid-thirties. Once you begin work as a doctor, you will constantly have an individual's life in your hands, daily, causing many instances of pressure. However, as a doctor, you must be *comfortable* being *uncomfortable* to assure your sanity is preserved and your patient's status is meticulously attended.

Life is not easy, and becoming successful, in conjunction with dealing with the struggles of life, can cause very uncomfortable situations. How you deal with these occurrences is what determines the level of success you will achieve. The higher you aim, the larger the aperture of successes that will presented to you. Adversely, a low aim will result in limited success opportunities being presented to you.

Do not only share your successes. Be transparent and share your failures as well. The key to not repeating history is to learn from it.

No one is perfect. Therefore, to only share the positive aspects of your life with people is a disservice to yourself, as well as the listener. Far too often, people only hear the good things that are accomplished as a result of your hard work. The failures that occurred throughout the process leading to success are hardly ever discussed.

To fully understand the journey to success in its entirety, you must know the vulnerabilities and setbacks that exist along your path. Understanding what caused these potential delays in the past will help you avoid making the same mistake again.

If you do not learn from history, you are doomed to repeat it. Repeating history, even when information is available to help mitigate it, is an unacceptable step in the overall process to becoming successful.

Never take no for an answer. Doing so would be submitting to failure, and failure is not an option.

If you truly believe in something and are not immediately successful during your journey, keep striving to complete your mission, no matter how many times you fail.

On your path to accomplishing your goal, there will be trials and tribulations that may discourage your motivation. If you are not successful at your first opportunity, continue to push forward until you shatter all expectations, including your own.

Eliminate the phrase "I can't" and the word "no" from your vocabulary and replace them with "I can do anything I want" and "yes I will," respectively. The confidence in knowing you have the ability and skill to accomplish your goal is half the battle. Becoming a successful entity is more of a state of mind than the actual physical talent or goal you want to achieve.

Battle's Application

I was a 23-year-old recent college graduate and newly commissioned officer in the Air Force. I received orders to move to Warner Robins, Georgia for my first duty assignment. I had the option to rent an apartment or buy a house, and after much research, I decided to step out of my comfort zone and purchase my first house for $69,000.

Initially, I was scared. It was the largest purchase I had made up to that point in my life. Although my mortgage payment was cheaper than many of the rental prices of the neighboring apartments, I feared the responsibility of owning my own place.

BATTLE'S BLUEPRINT

During my first summer in the new house, my air conditioner stopped working. I immediately began to wonder if I had made the right decision. My initial emotions of fear turned into disgust in myself for buying a house, rather than renting a place to live in.

When the air conditioner technician came to my house, he informed me that my compressor had failed and I needed to replace it. That was a quick $600 down the drain, but the work had to be accomplished if I wanted to stay cool during the hot central Georgia heat.

I had owned my house for less than a year and was already partially regretting my decision; however, over the course of my four-year stay in Georgia, I did not have any other major problems with my house. What I initially thought of as a failure, eventually became one of my greatest successes. I was able to eventually pay off the remaining balance of the mortgage 9 years later, while simultaneously renting it out to tenants; allowing the house to become another source of income for my family. My homebuying process brought me through many ups-and-downs; from helping me overcome my fear of responsibility to turning my perceived initial purchase "failure" into a profitable

lifelong successful acquisition.

BLUEPRINT #2: Outgrow Your Environment

Do not become a victim of your environment; outgrow it. Your environment does not shape your reality.

DO YOU SOMETIMES FEEL AS THOUGH, no matter how hard you try, your environment will dictate the level of success you will obtain? If you reside in a poor inner-city neighborhood or a rural community deprived of an abundance amount of opportunities to advance, do you feel as though there is no way to escape the normality surrounding you?

Although your environment influences your mindset, it does not decide your fate. YOU determine your destiny and how successful YOU will be. Your environment is just a place your body resides throughout your life. Your mental fortitude is what will drive you to overcome the adversities of your surroundings.

The purpose of life is surviving to become as successful as you can, in spite of the hardships life throws at you. The realities of life will present themselves; however, you cannot succumb to the valleys those hardships will unveil. You can still change and mature as an individual, while maintaining the same characteristics that shaped your foundation, because you mature on mental and spiritual levels as time progresses.

This principle is not just focused on less-developed environments. It applies to all environments and circumstances. To become successful and elevate yourself above your peers, you must mentally outgrow them. If you can become the most mentally tough and mature individual, you will possess the ability to ascend to any occasion presented to you because you have prepared yourself for that moment.

BATTLE'S BLUEPRINT
Do not live in the moment. Discover your talent and invest in your craft.

To acquire more out of life, you must invest in yourself. Ownership is key. Whether that ownership is in the form of real estate, a physical product or an investment in your future, such as a retirement account or stocks, it is imperative that you "bet" on yourself.

You must believe in yourself and be willing to take a risk on whatever talent you possess. Your talent does not have to be elaborate. It can be as simple as detailing vehicles or as complicated as developing software code as a computer scientist or engineer. In both instances, you can slowly create your own empire by investing in your talent. As a software coder, you can create your own website design business. You have the ability to offer a service to a potential customer who may not know how to structure software code and build a website. As a vehicle detailer, you can create a business and deliver a commodity that any able-bodied person is capable of doing but may not want to do or have the time to perform the task. Your unique capability of performing a simple task can become an opportunity to create something of OWNERSHIP for yourself.

You must invest in YOURSELF. If you are not willing to take a chance on your vision, then how can you expect anyone else to invest in YOUR dream? Investing in the knowledge and skills necessary to allow you to progress to a path of OWNERSHIP will pay huge dividends throughout your life. Money comes and goes. Fancy cars and *material things* are not permanent fixtures. But acquiring the knowledge and skills that will allow you to initiate the processes to become self-sufficient, no matter how dire the situation, is priceless. It brings about mental awareness and stability in knowing that you are never "down-and-out." You will be able to overcome any circumstance due to your initial investments in your skill and the knowledgebase of your talent.

Never make real decisions based on emotions.

Successful individuals are continuously on the *right* side of decision-making. You should never let anger, sadness, or anxiety impel you to make an unguided decision. If you are not careful, you can risk losing everything using such irrational judgement.

BATTLE'S BLUEPRINT

Before making a decision, it is important to step away from the situation and logically consider the benefits and disadvantages the decision will render. Challenge yourself to think outside of your isolated train of thought. Ask yourself what the secondary and tertiary effects of the decision are and whether it is truly necessary for you to proceed at this moment. Be honest with yourself during your assessment. If it is beneficial for you and all involved, then press forward. If not, do not let your emotions dictate the outcome.

If time permits, never make an impulsive decision. When your emotions are at their peak is the absolute worst time to decide what is best for you in a situation. At that moment, your reasoning and judgement are skewed, causing your thought process to be abnormal. Allow yourself enough time to reason with your suggested solution before making a decision.

Successful individuals are strategic in their decision making process. The ability to strategize decisions to result in favorable outcomes for all parties involved is what separates successful and non-successful individuals.

Never acquire things you do not need to impress people you do not like.

Many tend to believe that once you become successful, you must buy things that *successful* people acquire. This is the absolute wrong answer. You became successful being YOU, so why change that?

The purpose of becoming successful is to assure that you thrust yourself into a position in which you understand the difference between a *need* and a *want*. I'm not saying that you should not upgrade certain circumstances in your life. What I am suggesting is that you ask yourself *why* you are acquiring these things.

If the acquisition of an item is out of necessity, then purchasing it is an absolute yes. If the attainment of the item is a *want*, then you should think of the reasoning behind the purchase. If it is something that you truly want for personal reasons then purchase it, as long as your needs are met. If your reason to purchase the item is because you saw another person with it, or thought it would be the topic of discussion among social circles, then the item is not for you.

BATTLE'S BLUEPRINT

Living to impress others is expensive and detracts from your overall objective of becoming successful. If you are constantly acquiring items you do not want or need in order to impress others, you will eventually find yourself in a position of vulnerability, where you will do almost anything to gain attention and notoriety. Successful individuals are comfortable being themselves. Materialism and outside validation do not determine your level of success; rather, investing in yourself to assure your messages and talents have a purpose are what ultimately determines what success is.

Keep your goals in sight and strive to attain them. Once you conquer your prize, remember why you did it and most importantly, do not compromise yourself for anyone.

Tough times don't last...tough people do.

Challenges will occur throughout your life; however, they will pass, just as the sun sets and rises. The one constant force that will present itself to you on a day-to-day basis is YOU.

Tough times are ahead, and in order to be successful in life, you must prevail and fight through your circumstances. The difficult situation you are currently experiencing is not permanent. Every tough period you have previously experienced is more than likely a non-existent factor in your current life. Over time, the difficult period will eventually dissolve itself.

Additionally, some difficult events you encounter will lay a foundation and prepare you to handle the even tougher challenges you may face in the future. Although the events may seem like tall hurdles and impossible tasks to overcome, once completed, your mental toughness will be strong enough to withstand any trials that you will face in the future.

Battle's Application

I grew up in a lower income neighborhood in Shreveport, Louisiana. My mother was an 18-year-old single parent. We didn't have much at all, but we made the best of our situation.

Growing up, I saw, up-close and personal, the effects drugs could have on a family. With multiple people within my immediate family succumbing to the evils of drugs, I could have easily followed their footsteps and experimented with using and selling narcotics. However, my mental makeup was stronger than that of the environment surrounding me.

BATTLE'S BLUEPRINT

Drug dealers were rooted in my family just as basketball players were entrenched on an NBA team. They drove the nicest of cars, dated the prettiest of women, and made more money in a week than my mother made in a year. The temptations of *giving in* and following their footsteps would have been the easy way to fast money...as well as an easy way to prison or a life in a casket. When times got tough, my mental strength gave me the courage to keep my head high, even during a time of need.

That same strength pushed me to outgrow my environment and outpace the rate of success, or lack thereof, in my community. It pushed me to attend college. It drove me to join the military. Moreover, it led me to become an author, sharing my story in an effort to help YOU navigate through life's challenges.

Continue to be YOURSELF. Although it may be a tall task, block out as many negative influences as possible. Grow within yourself and mature throughout your journey. Trust your process and lead by example. Allow others the opportunity to see, through your actions, what success looks like.

BLUEPRINT #3: Understand Your Brilliance

The key to being successful is not simply understanding your brilliance. It's understanding how to use your brilliance to affect others.

DO YOU SOMETIMES STRUGGLE TO understand what your true talent is? Do not be ashamed if you do not know what you are great at. Some people know early in life what they were born to do. Others discover what gift they will contribute to this world later on in life. Whatever your special ability is, you need to understand that you must hone your craft to perfection and share it to the masses.

BATTLE'S BLUEPRINT

You have a unique talent within you that exudes brilliance. To be successful, you need to cultivate that talent in order to harvest the fruits of your brilliance. Once identified, you must use your brilliance in a fashion that will foster collaboration between you and others.

Brilliance is not recognized unless its application is known. If your idea or concept is truly magnificent, to fully become effective, it must be shared among others. Once distributed to the masses, it will have an overwhelming success if properly applied. If you are the originator of this brilliant act, you may want to take close-hold of it; however, repeat the quote below when you struggle with sharing your vision.

"50% of something is better than 100% of nothing."
– Suze Orman –

Your vision must grow in order for you to be successful. Yes, you may have created a brilliant piece of work. Yes, you constructed your dream with minimum assistance. But, as individuals, we tend to severely limit ourselves when it comes to our brilliance. You will definitely need to share your vision in order to allow constructive feedback and growth of your brilliant idea. No single person can achieve everything alone. Do not miss your opportunity to increase your vision's presence by being too arrogant to allow growth through sharing and partnership.

Do not conform to ignorance. Educate yourself on subjects you are unfamiliar with and continue to build your knowledge base by acquiring more information on subjects you are familiar with.

Education is one of the most successful tools you can have in your toolbox. Although many think of education as going to school, sitting in a classroom, and absorbing information, I deem that method of education as *certificate* completion activities. I'm not saying "Do not go to school." I am merely saying that formal classroom education is not for everyone.

Education can come in many forms. It is not only learning from educational institutions; it is also learning from your life experiences. In many instances, life experiences may be better learning opportunities than sitting in a *classroom*. For instance, if you fail a class, no worries. You have the opportunity to retake the course. In life, you may encounter instances in which you cannot fail. Learning how to navigate these circumstances so that you do not place yourself in this position again, may be more "educational" than the three-hour class you attend twice a week while attending school.

You may not be able to afford or have the opportunity to attend college; however, that does not dictate your education level. A wise man once told me that there are plenty of intelligent people who have never attended a day of college. On the contrary, there are also plenty of dumb individuals who have degrees (certificates). Do not let your lack of opportunities discourage you from becoming an *educated* individual.

Learning is not delegated to just the classroom. To fully digest the material, you must have open dialogue to promote better insight into the subject matter.

First off, "the classroom" is a figurative symbol for a place of learning. It's not literal in the sense of being educated within a school. In fact, the classroom is any place you can learn information. It can be your place of business, a social club meeting, barbershop, family reunion, etc. The classroom is essentially any place where you can learn something new.

When you gain new knowledge, you subconsciously view the new material through your eyes only. To begin the initial stages of learning the information, you tend to look at how it applies to your life and, in turn, base your understanding of the material in reference to your life experiences.

Although these are outstanding ways to grasp an overarching meaning of the information received, to fully immerse yourself with the new information, you must engage in open dialogue with those who may have differing views. Viewing the information through the lens of another person will ultimately allow you to increase your knowledge base of the subject.

Understanding an issue fully will allow you to think and speak intelligently on the topic. Intelligent dialogue will promote a healthy acceptance of the views displayed within the information in its entirety, even if you do not agree with another person's interpretation of the subject.

Process over Results

In order to succeed, you have to practice the techniques necessary for success so frequently that you cannot mess them up, even if you want to. This method of learning to succeed is often used in sports, as evident with the quarterback position in football.

A football quarterback is taught the correct throwing motion from the moment he/she begins playing the sport. Usually, by the time the player has reached college, or even the NFL, the throwing motion they have been taught over the past 15 years is not going to change much at all. Their repetitive muscle memory will not allow them to naturally break its habit.

In relation to everyday life, you want to be able to complete successful mental muscle memory techniques to the extent that your mind and body know exactly what to do when it is time to succeed. When going through the process of achieving success, times of strife will occur. When they do, you will revert back to what you automatically know how to accomplish, without having to mentally process your actions. The Greek poet Archilochus claimed, "We don't rise to the level of our expectations, we fall to the level of our training." Make sure YOU are trained properly.

Although there might be a faster way to get the results that you immediately want, sometimes you have to stay the course and continue your daily regimen to sustained success. You have to remember to not only be results-oriented. Moreover, you must trust the process. Do not ask yourself if things have worked out. Instead, you should ask yourself if you made the right decisions en route to achieving your outcome. Trust your process and the results that come with it.

Proceeding with a results-oriented approach may seem like the best method to achieve success; however, you must rely on your maturity and self-awareness in order to remain consistent. Do not beat yourself up if something goes wrong. Trust the process and your team surrounding you that will propel you to success. Just remember that instant gratification is not attainable for every aspect of your life. The majority of instances will require you to trust the proven techniques that will render long term success. Have faith in the process and continue to enjoy success!

Battle's Application

As a youth, math was my brilliance. If it had to do with numbers, I was intrigued by it. My grandmother realized this and began bringing mathematic books to her house for me to work on during the weekends I spent with her. By the time I was in the 5th grade, I was completing math problems on a 9th grade level.

Obviously, math became my favorite subject. I was intrigued by algebra, calculus, and trigonometry. I always received an 'A' in these classes. My fondness for the subject led me to complete three college equivalent courses while still in high school. My love for math steered me toward attending college as a mechanical engineering student.

Although I was talented with numbers, I began to think of ways I could transfer my knowledge to others. I thought of many ways to do this but could not figure out a means to accomplish this until I met Mrs. Barbara Johnson. She was the lead coordinator of an Austin, Texas based tutoring program called Partners In Education (PIE).

I tutored local youth every Tuesday for the last three years of my college career alongside my fraternity brothers and many college friends. During this time, we accelerated these children's math learning curve, as well as that of various other subjects. The program led me to also partake in a similar program at my first duty station in the Air Force at Warner Robins, Georgia.

Succeeding in math and earning a degree in mechanical engineering was a great accomplishment; however, paying my knowledge base forward to future generations meant so much more. It was as gratifying of an accomplishment that I have ever felt.

Outside of the classroom, I still continued to educate myself in math. As a sports fan, I became intrigued with sports analytics, especially when it pertained to football. I always wondered how analysts created their formulas to track specific football player metrics. Most of the formulas are never shared and are marked proprietary to its creator.

Since I was not privy to the information within these formulas, I decided to create my own formula. I taught myself how to create a formula that tracked a football team or player efficiency ratings. I wrestled with creating the formula for over six months. I crafted my formula from reviewing football film and stats. I did not need a "standard" classroom to teach me how to create this formula. I created my own classroom within my house and educated myself on what was important to create my metric. I educated myself on an unfamiliar subject matter. Once I felt as though I had immersed myself in the correct information necessary to create a relevant formula, I continued to learn how to decipher what stats were most important to the creation of my successful metric.

After creating my formula, I was able to apply it within a sports agency to assist in selecting players for the company to represent. It was a success and truly validated and verified my work.

I did not attend college for data or business analytics; however, they were subjects that I wanted to learn more about. After garnering as much information concerning analytics as possible, I was able to expand upon my brilliance in the subject…a brilliance I did not know I possessed until later in life.

Everything you desire may not come immediately to you. In many instances, things will appear as you begin to learn more about yourself. Do not become discouraged when acting upon your learning desires. Remain focused and continue to immerse yourself in learning. Continuous learning is great at limiting periods of discouragement and is healthy for your mental well-being.

BLUEPRINT #4: Respect Your Relationships

Respect and understanding lead to mutual respect for one another. Mutual respect leads to the peaceful coexistence necessary for a successful relationship.

HAVE YOU EVER WORKED IN AN environment where you were constantly at odds with your co-workers, teammates, subordinates, and/or leadership? Have you ever felt as though you could do your job better without these individuals? Although you may think you would be better off working independently, you will soon find out that the work of a unified team usually exceeds that of a single person, nearly every time across the life of the project you work on.

There is no successful businessman or businesswoman who has done it by themselves. In order to reach your ultimate heights, you must work well with others. Whatever field you choose to work in, you will either have people working below or above you…or possibly both. You will also interact with peers within your industry. Maintaining mutually respectful relationships will foster an environment suitable for success.

You must be honest and compassionate towards those you have relationships with. Understand that a disagreement is not an argument. It's only a difference of opinions, and these instances are not worth losing valuable working relationships, mentors, leaders, and in many cases, friends.

To succeed in life, you must respect others, even if they are in opposition to your message. Exhibiting a strong willingness to be open-minded, while maintaining outstanding mutual relationships, will pay dividends in your journey to living a successful life.

Dissect the degrees of separation and understand who has your best interest in mind.

Understanding who has your best interest in mind is not just taking someone's words as truth. It is observing the actions of these individuals towards you in the midst of any situation. A person that has your best interest in mind will do what is best for you, no matter the situation. If you need to make a decision on an important matter, they will present all options to you, even if some may not be your preference.

Having a person's best interest in mind is guiding them to an attainable solution that will have the least amount of catastrophic failure to you. It is uncovering hidden innuendos within a decision-making process in order to discover unforeseen potential problems. Determining troubled areas is not an easy task. You must remain committed to excellence and success in order to continually sift problematic solutions from valuable ones.

If you have a person's best interest in mind, you essentially become a mock employee to that individual. Your job is to not allow that person to make a decision that may be detrimental to their success. These same characteristics should be applied to someone who vouches to have your back in the heat of the moment. Just assure that you use these same principles when you employ them as a potential supervisor.

Sometimes, you have to make a hard decision even when you do not want to.

As simple as this statement may sound, it is often the most underrated and overlooked success principle that exists. Making hard decisions is not easy to accomplish. Emotions, relationships, and fear of change can drive you to not make the *right* decision at the *right* moment.

You may be achieving success at a relatively high level; however, successful individuals are not content with the level they are currently at. Although you are thriving in success, you should always strive to become more extraordinary than you already are. Was Bill Gates, Oprah Winfrey, or Warren Buffett content with making their first million dollars? Or first hundred million dollars? Or first billion dollars? The answer to this question is no, evidenced by their constant progression throughout their successful lives.

BATTLE'S BLUEPRINT

Speaking of Buffett, he has previously stated that no matter how much he is in favor of a decision, if he does not feel comfortable with the decision being written about and discussed the next day in his local newspaper, he makes the hard decision to not press forward with the action. No matter how much money the decision will net or how much joy it will bring to yourself or your associates, your reputation will supersede all. The difficult decision to not press forward with this action is warranted and necessary to maintain, which is what safeguards the level of success Buffett has attained.

Hard decisions are difficult to make; however, before making one, you should step back, take a breath, and gather your thoughts to make the most logical decision. Take your emotions out of the situation and think in broader terms. Ask yourself how this decision will not only affect you, but also those around you. Additionally, think in terms of how this decision will benefit you and others for years to come. Do not make the easy decision of what is most beneficial at the current moment. Assess the importance of how your decision will potentially affect the masses for years to come.

NICHOLAS BATTLE
Unorganized chaos results in detrimental conflict. Detrimental conflict results in negative profit margins.

First off, profit margins represent not only money, but also the savings of *success* deposited into your life's bank account. They are merely a metaphor for accomplishment and achievement. They are the necessary actions for continued progression within yourself.

At some moment within your voyage to a successful life, you will partake in moments of chaos that will test your inner strength, will and determination. The key to being successful is learning how to take on and manage this chaos.

When you hear the word chaos related to being successful, you think of an unfavorable word. I will argue that chaos is not a negative term. As a military member with tours to Iraq and Afghanistan, each morning I woke up in these countries was a moment of complete chaos. I was in another country, away from my family, and outside of the comforts I had become accustomed to.

Although the situation was chaotic, it was organized. I deem it as *organized chaos* because, even though the environment was hectic, in order for our nation to be successful, we had to be detailed oriented and structured to survive. On the flip side, if we were unorganized, the specific missions and tasks we were to complete might have failed, causing the possibility of failure within our unit. A failed unit has the potential to cripple neighboring units, which in turn will decrease the safety of our nation. Although this example may seem like the most pessimistic illustration of *unorganized chaos*, it is definitely a reality for the situation at hand.

If you apply these same principles to business and life, you will realize that managing and navigating through chaos is an absolute necessity. As long as you set parameters and have order within yourself, these periods of chaos will be brief, merely minor speedbumps throughout your excursion. If, however, you cannot manage the chaos presented to you and begin to live in a life of *unorganized chaos*, your *profit margins* will dwindle and your chances of success will become scarce.

Battle's Application

When my mother first married my stepfather, I immediately resisted everything concerning the marriage. I did not want to leave my hometown of Shreveport, Louisiana to eventually wind up living in Killeen, Texas. My anger at leaving Shreveport caused me to dislike everything about Killeen, including my stepfather.

It wasn't that I actually disliked my stepfather, it was the notion that I believed he was the only reason why I had to leave my family and comfort zone in Shreveport. I fought and cried to leave Texas and go back to Shreveport. My stepfather stood tall and steady. He continually preached to me that Texas was the best place for me, but I did not want to hear anything he was saying.

Eventually, after continued resistance to living in Texas, my stepfather sat me down and told me how much he cared for and loved me. He assured me that he was going to remain in my corner for the rest of my life.

At that moment, I knew he had my best interests at the forefront of his mind at all times. For that reason, not only did I have a great amount of love for my stepfather, but I respected him much more because he made the hard decision to stand fast and absorb my verbal lashes of being unhappy. He knew I was only expressing temporary emotions due to the extreme changes in my life conditions. Our mutual respect for each other led to a peaceful and loving father-son relationship that continues to last

and grow with each passing day.

BLUEPRINT #5: Maintain a Healthy Work/Life Balance

Reclaim control of your life by maintaining a healthy work/life balance.

ARE THE STRESSES OF WORK INTERFERING with the time you spend with your family? Do you constantly struggle with knowing when to not think about work? We all strive to accomplish the highest of achievements at work; however, we should also attempt to do the same within our household.

To become successful, you must allocate your time appropriately across your work environment and other areas of your life. A healthy work/life balance will keep you mentally strong. Instead on being overworked and losing your mind, an overall equal share between the challenges of work and the joys of life will allow you to loosen your mind, in an effort to become mentally refreshed.

To balance the work portion of your schedule, you need to strive to become more efficient on a daily basis. The better you prioritize your time, the more efficient you will be. In order to maintain efficiency, set miniature milestones within your daily routine that will assure you accomplish the task you set for yourself. Completing these tasks within specified deadlines will keep you on schedule to finishing your assigned task on time.

Balancing your home life should be the easier of the two activities to control. Unfortunately, it is usually the most difficult. As a hardworking and dedicated individual, you never want to leave unfinished business at work for the next day. Far too often, you continue to work on your job duties while you should be enjoying your spare time at home.

The emergence of technology allows you to continue your work at home; however, you should concentrate on a means to eliminate this. Once you get home, place your cell phone on a table opposite of you in the room you occupy. This will allow you to resist the temptation to check for text messages or linked work email accounts on your phone.

Additionally, with the majority of jobs requiring access to computers, try to limit your home computer access. Instead of reaching for your computer or tablet while at home, grab a book or magazine to stimulate your mind while you relax. Read to your children or take a walk around the neighborhood with a friend or spouse. Your body, mind and soul will thank you for it.

Battle's Application

During my military assignment in Los Angeles, California, I was selected to become an Executive Officer to a 2-Star General. My job duties entailed essentially being the right-hand man to the General Officer. I had to keep him on schedule and make sure he attended all his meetings on time. Another one of my duties was to assure he was abreast of all issues that were occurring at our duty station.

I showed up at work before he arrived and left after he exited the building. Some days were rougher than others; however, nearly 12 hours of my day was associated with my keeping my boss on track.

Initially, I struggled with bringing work home. I would always check my work-issued cell phone to assure any incoming emails would be answered if need be. I neglected time with my family to guarantee my job was done to the utmost of my ability. But honestly, I should have been guaranteeing my family had my undivided attention during my time at home.

One Saturday afternoon, I took my family out to dinner, but the only thing I paid attention to was my work cell phone. I checked emails constantly and payed less attention to my family than the phone in front of me. My wife grew extremely agitated and I could not figure out the reason until she told me exactly what I was doing wrong.

Initially, I denied her claims but after thinking about what she told me, I knew she was right. It was a slow process, but I eventually balanced my work-life environment to assure my work was accomplished and my personal relationships were satisfied. I began to realize that the majority of the work I stressed about was still going to be waiting for me the next day.

After a couple of deployments to Afghanistan and Iraq, I understood the importance of priority. No one was going to die if a document was not signed at 10:00PM on a Tuesday night to approve a minor task on base. It could wait until the morning. There was no need to sacrifice time away from my wife and child during our quality time moments to answer something that my boss would not see until the following day.

I learned to enjoy my time with my family even more than before. A healthy family relationship and home environment paid huge dividends toward producing a better quality of work throughout the week. Satisfaction at both home and work is essential to succeeding on both fronts. Enjoy and thrive in both.

Acknowledgments

First, I have to thank the Man above for all his blessings. This book would not have been possible without His guidance.

A special thank you goes to my beautiful wife for encouraging me to share my truths with you all. Love you sweetie.

To my son Landon, you make me a better man. Being your father is the absolute greatest thing I have ever accomplished in life. Love you buddy.

To my Mom and Larry, I would not be here without the great foundation set for me. I pay forward the principles you taught me to Landon, your grandchild and butter-bean, every day. Thank you and love you.

To my great friend, Charlynda Scales, thank YOU so much for composing the foreword for this book. It means the world to me.

I have had the pleasure of having great leaders that helped mold me into the successful man I am today. I had a ton of educators who helped shape me, primarily my 5th grade teacher, Mrs. Patricia Beauchamp, my elementary school principal, Mrs. Linda Cox, and my high school drafting teacher, Mr. Nate Moses.

I have the pleasure of serving with some of the greatest men and women across all Military Services and Department of Defense agencies in this country. Thank you Lieutenant General (Ret.) Samuel Greaves, Lieutenant General Robert McMurry, Brigadier General Ryan Britton, Brigadier General (Ret.) Mark Baird, Brigadier General (Ret.) Carl Buhler, Colonel John "Chop" Frazier, Colonel (Ret.) Scott Fike, Colonel (Ret.) Cheryl "C.A." Allen, Colonel (Ret.) Rodney Couick, Colonel (Ret.) Meryl Tengesdal, Colonel Alvin Burse, Colonel Glen Santos, Mr. John Morris, Mrs. Ratna Ramirez, Mrs. Mary Rich, Mrs. Lisa Hague-McDonald, Lieutenant Colonel Mark Lewis, Lieutenant Colonel Geno Burton, Lieutenant Colonel Natasha Miller, Lieutenant Colonel Rob Yates, Lieutenant Colonel Jeromie Shoulders, Lieutenant Colonel Jesse Moreno, Lieutenant Colonel Niece Vandyke, Major Robert Jobe, Major Jeff Hoover, Major Johnny Lynum, Mr. Kelley Thompson, Mr. Ronald Major, and the many other members I have served with. It has been an absolute pleasure.

Additional titles from Nicholas "NinosCorner" Battle

Can U Love Me: A Memoir…A Tribute

5-Time #1 Best Seller

For booking information, contact:
Email: TheNinosCorner@gmail.com
Website: www.NinosCorner.com

About the Author

 **NICHOLAS BATTLE** is bestselling author of the beloved book, *Can U Love Me: A Memoir…A Tribute.* Battle is a military officer, who has served as lead for numerous Program Management and Engineering positions both in the continental United States and while deployed to locations in Iraq and Afghanistan in support of Operation Iraqi and Operation Enduring Freedom. Battle received a Master of Science (M.S.) degree in Technology Intelligence, with a specialization in Cyber and Data Analytics, from the National Intelligence University, a M.S. degree in Industrial Technology from Texas A&M-Commerce, and a Bachelor of Science degree in Mechanical Engineering from the University of Texas. He also received a Graduate Certificate in Sports Industry Essentials from Columbia University. Battle founded NinosCorner Productions, a production company for music, books and film. He also founded BattleStat Sports, a data analytics company that provides football player and team evaluations to sports agencies. Battle currently resides in Fairfax, VA, with his wife Lillian and son Landon. Discover more at NinosCorner.com.